Scoring High

Stanford Achievement Test

A Test Prep Program

Book 2

SRA

Columbus, OH

The **McGraw-Hill** Companies

www.sra4kids.com

 SRA

Send all inquiries to:
SRA/McGraw-Hill
4400 Easton Commons
Columbus, OH 43219

ISBN 0-07-584095-2

10 11 12 13 14 BCM 13 12 11 10 09

The **McGraw·Hill** Companies

Book 2 On Your Way to Scoring High Stanford Achievement Test

Name _____

Word Study Skills

Lesson 1a Word Study Skills

SAMPLE A

basement	carpet	airplane
○	○	○

TIP If you are not sure which answer choice is correct, take your best guess.

1

drawer	hotdog	reason
○	○	○

4

unhappy	highway	handle
○	○	○

2

horseback	pottery	rabbit
○	○	○

5

whisper	blanket	grapefruit
○	○	○

3

sparkle	thirsty	cowboy
○	○	○

6

showboat	hidden	driver
○	○	○

STOP

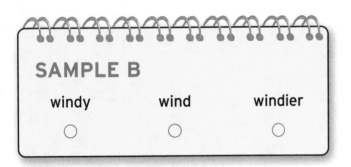

SAMPLE B

windy	wind	windier
○	○	○

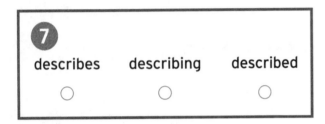

7

describes	describing	described
○	○	○

8

trading	trades	trader
○	○	○

9

slowest	slowly	slower
○	○	○

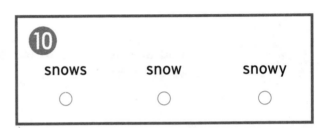

10

snows	snow	snowy
○	○	○

11

teaching	teach	teachers
○	○	○

12

shortly	shortest	shorter
○	○	○

STOP

SAMPLE C

haven't	hasn't	hadn't
○	○	○

13

he's	he'd	he'll
○	○	○

16

couldn't	should've	shouldn't
○	○	○

14

weren't	wasn't	won't
○	○	○

17

isn't	wasn't	hasn't
○	○	○

15

didn't	don't	doesn't
○	○	○

18

she'd	she'll	she's
○	○	○

STOP

Word Study Skills

Lesson 1b **Word Study Skills**

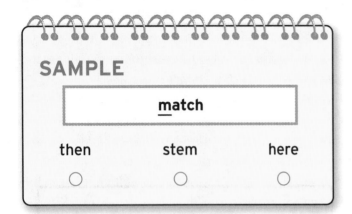

SAMPLE

match

then   stem   here
○   ○   ○

Say each word to yourself. Listen for the sound of the underlined part.

1
chip

cost   reach   hit
○   ○   ○

2
toy

buy   say   oil
○   ○   ○

3
defend

wander   lunch   need
○   ○   ○

4
fine

list   dry   chief
○   ○   ○

5
friend

scarf   frost   raft
○   ○   ○

GO

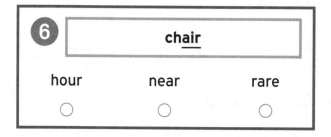

6 **ch_ai_r**

hour   near   rare
○   ○   ○

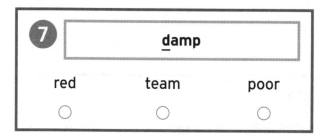

7 **_d_amp**

red   team   poor
○   ○   ○

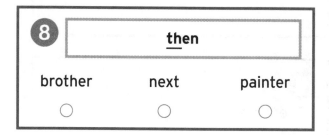

8 **_th_en**

brother   next   painter
○   ○   ○

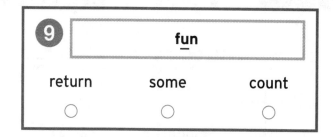

9 **f_un_**

return   some   count
○   ○   ○

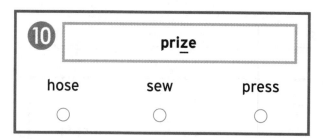

10 **pri_z_e**

hose   sew   press
○   ○   ○

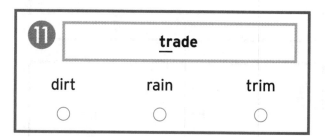

11 **_tr_ade**

dirt   rain   trim
○   ○   ○

Test Yourself: Word Study Skills

SAMPLE A

lightbulb	mountain	certain
○	○	○

SAMPLE B

bowling	bowls	bowler
○	○	○

1

music	seaweed	instead
○	○	○

2

shadow	between	paintbrush
○	○	○

3

wildcat	correct	report
○	○	○

4

baseball	farmer	practice
○	○	○

5

drawing	draws	draw
○	○	○

6

friends	friend	friendlier
○	○	○

7

safer	safe	safety
○	○	○

8

harder	hardly	hardy
○	○	○

STOP

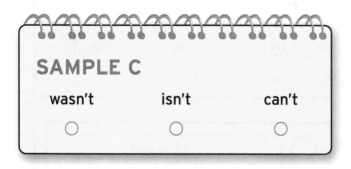

SAMPLE C

wasn't   isn't   can't

○   ○   ○

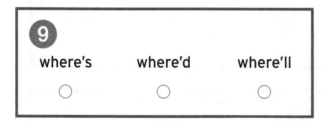

9

where's   where'd   where'll

○   ○   ○

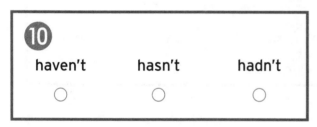

10

haven't   hasn't   hadn't

○   ○   ○

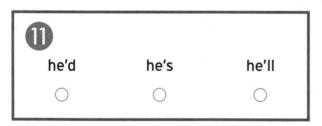

11

he'd   he's   he'll

○   ○   ○

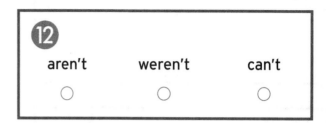

12

aren't   weren't   can't

○   ○   ○

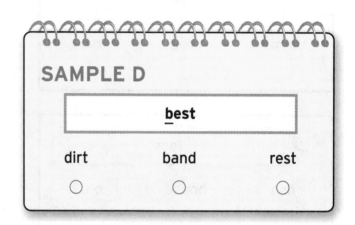

SAMPLE D

<u>b</u>est

dirt   band   rest

○   ○   ○

13

m<u>ee</u>t

mend   read   heart

○   ○   ○

GO ➡

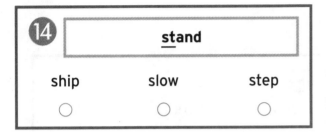

14 **stand**

ship	slow	step
○	○	○

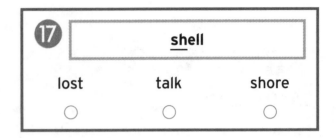

17 **shell**

lost	talk	shore
○	○	○

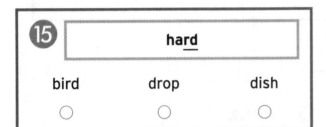

15 **hard**

bird	drop	dish
○	○	○

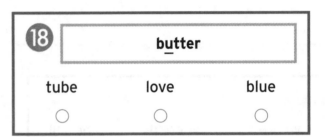

18 **butter**

tube	love	blue
○	○	○

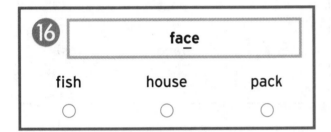

16 **face**

fish	house	pack
○	○	○

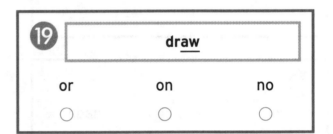

19 **draw**

or	on	no
○	○	○

STOP

SAMPLE A

> To <u>listen</u> is to —

- ○ see
- ○ feel
- ○ hear
- ○ think

SAMPLE B

> <u>Silent</u> means —

- ○ stiff
- ○ quiet
- ○ friendly
- ○ plain

Skip hard items and come back to them later.

1 | <u>Below</u> means —

- ○ beside
- ○ around
- ○ above
- ○ under

3 | A <u>chore</u> is a —

- ○ game
- ○ visit
- ○ job
- ○ seat

2 | Something that is <u>true</u> is not —

- ○ false
- ○ short
- ○ long
- ○ sad

4 | A <u>flood</u> is a lot of —

- ○ dirt
- ○ water
- ○ snow
- ○ wind

GO ➡

5 | Something that is <u>hard</u> is —

○ a little late
○ not soft
○ lost
○ light

6 | <u>Dim</u> means —

○ not bright
○ nearby
○ small
○ not here

7 | To <u>pretend</u> is to —

○ join
○ make believe
○ argue
○ lose something

8 | A <u>section</u> is a —

○ town
○ part
○ path
○ vegetable

9 | <u>Dull</u> means not —

○ funny
○ happy
○ sad
○ bright

10 | A <u>frame</u> goes around a —

○ picture
○ room
○ field
○ car

11 | <u>Imaginary</u> means —

○ real
○ unusual
○ made up
○ rare

12 | A <u>dome</u> is a kind of —

○ wall
○ floor
○ roof
○ room

STOP

SAMPLE A

> She lost her <u>ring</u>.

In which sentence does the word <u>ring</u> mean the same thing as in the sentence above?

- ○ A glass can be made to <u>ring</u>.
- ○ We joined hands to form a <u>ring</u>.
- ○ Did you <u>ring</u> the doorbell?
- ○ A <u>ring</u> was on her finger.

SAMPLE B

> If you <u>hurry</u>, you can catch the bus. <u>Hurry</u> means —

- ○ shout
- ○ drive slowly
- ○ go fast
- ○ plan well

Use the meaning of the sentence to find the right answer.

1 | <u>Pick</u> up your clothes.

In which sentence does the word <u>pick</u> mean the same thing as in the sentence above?

- ○ Use a <u>pick</u> to break up the dirt.
- ○ This apple is the <u>pick</u> of the crop.
- ○ Jay volunteered to <u>pick</u> up trash.
- ○ We'll <u>pick</u> you up at noon.

2 | Be sure to <u>tie</u> the knot tightly.

In which sentence does the word <u>tie</u> mean the same thing as in the sentence above?

- ○ <u>Tie</u> the string around the papers.
- ○ This <u>tie</u> goes with that shirt.
- ○ The game ended in a <u>tie</u>.
- ○ We used a railroad <u>tie</u> for a step.

GO ➡

3 We'll have to brush the dirt off.

In which sentence does the word brush mean the same thing as in the sentence above?

○ This brush is too large for that job.

○ Joy will brush the leaves away.

○ We had a close brush with a bear.

○ The ball flew into the heavy brush.

4 The seal swam into the waves.

In which sentence does the word seal mean the same thing as in the sentence above?

○ The king's seal was on the scroll.

○ Seal the letter before mailing it.

○ Did you visit the seal tank?

○ The plastic bag has a tight seal.

5 Can Len recall the address? Recall means —

○ remember

○ find

○ write

○ explain

6 The bleachers are a good place to watch the game. Bleachers are —

○ players

○ tickets

○ shoes

○ seats

7 Water flowed from the spout. A spout is a kind of —

○ cloud

○ rock

○ opening

○ statue

8 We had a wonderful feast at Thanksgiving. A feast is a —

○ hike

○ telephone call

○ large meal

○ game

STOP

Test Yourself: Reading Vocabulary

SAMPLE A

To **combine** is to —

- ○ separate
- ○ mix together
- ○ search for
- ○ buy

SAMPLE B

To **shout** is to —

- ○ yell
- ○ push
- ○ lift
- ○ move

1 To **celebrate** is to —

- ○ have a party
- ○ go to sleep
- ○ play a game
- ○ find something

2 A **lodge** is a —

- ○ field
- ○ building
- ○ lake
- ○ mountain

3 **Pleasant** means —

- ○ nice
- ○ soft
- ○ huge
- ○ colorful

4 A **town** is a kind of —

- ○ club
- ○ city
- ○ river
- ○ show

STOP

13

SAMPLE C

> Place the book on the shelf.

In which sentence does the word place mean the same thing as in the sentence above?

- ○ Meet me at John's place.
- ○ Which place was the most fun?
- ○ Annie held my place in line.
- ○ Did you place the cup on the desk?

---

5 Whose turn is it?

In which sentence does the word turn mean the same thing as in the sentence above?

- ○ Shonto made a right turn.
- ○ Turn the radio on, please.
- ○ Remember to turn the page.
- ○ My turn comes after Winnie's.

---

6 The back of the room is noisy.

In which sentence does the word back mean the same thing as in the sentence above?

- ○ We will go back to the lake soon.
- ○ Milk is in the back of the store.
- ○ Can you back up a little?
- ○ Allen hurt his back swimming.

---

7 Give me a hand with this box.

In which sentence does the word hand mean the same thing as in the sentence above?

- ○ Karen cut her hand on a shell.
- ○ We were able to lend them a hand.
- ○ The crowd gave the team a hand.
- ○ Hand me that hammer, please.

STOP

SAMPLE D

My arm was <u>aching</u> after I bumped it. <u>Aching</u> means —

- ○ sore
- ○ weak
- ○ strong
- ○ wet

8 The <u>crane</u> landed in the pond. A <u>crane</u> is a kind of —

- ○ fish
- ○ turtle
- ○ frog
- ○ bird

9 It was an <u>ordinary</u> day in which nothing happened. <u>Ordinary</u> is —

- ○ busy
- ○ strange
- ○ normal
- ○ boring

10 Minora <u>attended</u> the Miller School. <u>Attended</u> means —

- ○ lived near
- ○ liked
- ○ left
- ○ went to

STOP

SAMPLES

Kids' Club

You and your friends can start your own club. Clubs can do things for fun. Clubs can also help others. These are some of the things you and your friends should think of before you start your club.

1. What will be the name of the club?
2. What is the purpose of the club? What will we want this club to do?
3. Who will run the club?
4. Who can join the club?
5. How will decisions be made?
6. When will we meet?
7. Where will we have our meetings?

SAMPLE A

Which of these must be decided before the first meeting?

○ Who will run the club?
○ What will the club be named?
○ Where will the meeting be held?
○ Who will be invited to join the club?

SAMPLE B

This list will help you —

○ play a new game
○ start a new club
○ do well in school
○ become a member of a team

"Skim" the story. Look back at the story to answer the questions. You don't have to memorize the story.

GO

Butterfly of Thailand

My friends and family call me Butterfly. It is my nickname. My real name is Kamon, and I live in Thailand. This is a country far away near China.

My home is on the water, on a canal called a klong. We go everywhere by small boats called sampans. We even go to school on a boat. Farmers take their fruits and vegetables to market by boat. We wash our clothes and take baths in the klong. Every child learns to swim.

My country is very beautiful. It is warm all year. Much rain falls here. My family celebrates many festivals and holidays with special dinners and trips. Many people like to visit Thailand.

1 This story was written <u>mainly</u> to —

○ tell what a place looks like
○ show how to do something
○ solve a problem
○ tell about how people live

3 What is the <u>best</u> way to learn more about <u>Thailand</u>?

○ Read a book about Thailand
○ Look up Thailand in the dictionary
○ Eat food from Thailand
○ Visit a canal

2 How does the family celebrate holidays?

○ By going to the Floating Market
○ With a meal and a trip
○ By resting
○ By playing sports

GO

Lost and Found

Bud's pet was a tiny, yellow bird named Emma. Every day he would open the door to Emma's cage and hold out his finger. The bird liked to hop on Bud's finger. She would turn her head to the side and look at him and say, "Tweet, tweet." She seemed to know that Bud was her friend.

Bud gave Emma seeds in a cup. He put pieces of apple in her cage. He gave her a long, white bone to sharpen her beak. He put some gravel in a cup for Emma. He made sure she had fresh water every day. At night he put a blanket over her cage. Sometimes Bud let Emma fly around the house.

One day, Emma was out of her cage flying around the house. Bud was cleaning the cage and putting in fresh seeds and water. Bud's brother opened the door to the house and forgot to close it. Emma flew outside before Bud could catch her.

"I am so sorry, Bud. I did not know Emma was out of the cage. I will help you find her," Bud's brother said.

The boys went all over the neighborhood. They called and called. They asked all the people if anyone had seen the little, yellow bird that said, "Tweet, tweet." No one had seen her.

The boys were very sad. Bud wanted to cry, but he did not. He thought he would never see his bird again.

GO

The next morning, their mother opened the door to get the newspaper. There, sitting on a bush, was Emma! "Bud, come here quickly," she called.

Bud put out his finger just as he did when he was taking Emma out of her cage. She hopped on his finger and let him carry her back into the house. She said "Tweet, tweet" and seemed very happy to be home.

All day long, Bud had a big smile on his face. In the future, he would always be extra careful whenever he cleaned Emma's cage.

4 How old is Bud?

○ Older than 10
○ 8
○ 7
○ The story does not say

5 This story is mainly about —

○ a boy and his bird
○ a boy who did something wrong
○ learning to care for a pet
○ searching but not finding

6 Why did Bud's mother call him when she saw the bird?

○ She did not know what to do to get the bird back.
○ She thought his brother might scare the bird away.
○ She thought Bud could catch Emma.
○ She was afraid the cat might get the bird.

STOP

SAMPLES

How Bandages Are Made

One of the best first-aid treatments is a bandage. A bandage will help a cut heal faster. It will also keep the cut clean and prevent infection.

Long ago, bandages were just strips of cloth. Later, people made the cloth sticky. Finally, pads were added to the sticky strips of cloth.

Today, most bandages are made of plastic. A special glue is put on the plastic, then it is cut into strips. Gauze pads are attached to the sticky side of the plastic. The gauze keeps the glue off the cut and protects it. As part of the process, bandages are put into a giant oven. They are heated to kill any germs on them. This means you can put a bandage on a cut and feel safe.

SAMPLE A

> What are most bandages made of today?

- ○ Cloth
- ○ Plastic
- ○ Cotton
- ○ Paper

SAMPLE B

> This story was written mainly to tell you —

- ○ when you should use a bandage
- ○ where you can buy bandages
- ○ how bandages are made
- ○ how to give first aid

GO ➡

Brave Tonga

Tonga was a furry, golden lion cub. He loved to run and play all day. When night came, Tonga stayed as close as he could to his mother. "I'm afraid of the dark, Mama. Stay right here by me, Mama," Tonga said every night.

When he got bigger, Tonga's mother talked to him about being afraid. She said that lions were brave. "Lions are not afraid of anything," she said.

During the day, Tonga agreed with her. At night, he still snuggled close to her side. He was still not convinced.

One night, Tonga heard a terrible sound and was afraid. He started to cry.

"Listen, Tonga. That is your father. He is roaring. He is the ruler of the jungle. "Now look at your claws, Son. You can pull them back in, but they are very sharp. Feel your teeth. They are strong and sharp. You are a lion. You are growing bigger. Soon you will go on a hunt," Tonga's mother said.

The next night, Tonga's mother told him to go out a little way into the jungle by himself. Tonga stayed out for a while and then came home. Each night, Tonga spent more time alone in the jungle. He listened to his father's roar and wasn't afraid. He heard other sounds and wasn't afraid.

One morning, some wild dogs came near Tonga and his mother. Without thinking, he ran up to them and let out a roar. It wasn't a very loud roar yet, but the wild dogs ran away. He stood as tall as he could and thought to himself, "I am not afraid. I have protected my mother. I am strong and brave. I am a lion." He let out another roar.

GO ➡

1 In the beginning of the story, Tonga did <u>not</u> like —

○ his mother

○ his father

○ the dark

○ the jungle

2 When Tonga first went out into the jungle by himself, he felt —

○ a little brave

○ sorry that he had been afraid before

○ weak and small

○ ready to go on a hunt by himself

3 By the end of the story, Tonga has learned to —

○ be afraid

○ act like a lion

○ roar as loudly as his father

○ hunt with the other grown lions

4 What will probably happen soon?

○ Tonga will teach other lion cubs not to be afraid of the dark.

○ Tonga will forget how to roar.

○ Tonga will go on a hunt with the other lions.

○ Tonga will be afraid of the wild dogs.

5 Another good name for this story is —

○ "Lions and Wild Dogs"

○ "Afraid of the Dark"

○ "The Funny Lion"

○ "Tonga Grows Up"

6 In this story, a <u>ruler</u> is like —

○ a measuring stick

○ a king

○ an enemy

○ a friend

STOP

Test Yourself: Reading Comprehension

Early Morning

Rita felt someone shaking her. She blinked her eyes and saw her father standing over her. Half-awake, she remembered this was the day they would go fishing in the river. She jumped out of bed and got ready quickly.

SAMPLE

This story is <u>mainly</u> about —

○ a father going fishing

○ a girl waking up

○ a family

○ a vacation

Sisters Sharing

"It is my piece of cake!" said Jane.

"I want some of it," said her sister Sue. "You must share with me."

"No, no, no, it is mine. I don't want to share with you," said Jane.

"Girls, stop fussing now," said their mother. "Jane, you must share. Sue shared with you yesterday. Don't you remember?"

Jane nodded. Sue smiled.

Mother said, "One of you will cut the piece of cake in two. The other one will have the first choice of pieces."

GO ➡

"I will cut," said Jane.

"Then I will choose first," said Sue.

Sue watched Jane carefully as she cut the cake into two even pieces. Sue picked one of them. Then they sat side by side and ate their cake.

"Isn't this good cake, Sue?" asked Jane.

"Yes, and I am glad that sisters share with each other," laughed Sue.

---

1 In this story, the person who has the piece of cake is —

- ○ Sue
- ○ Jane
- ○ Mother
- ○ Amy

2 What did Mother say that one of the girls should do first?

- ○ Choose the piece of cake she wanted
- ○ Cut the cake into two pieces
- ○ Eat the cake
- ○ Save the cake until after dinner

3 What will Sue and Jane probably do the next time there is just one piece of cake?

- ○ Argue over it
- ○ Share it
- ○ Save it to eat later
- ○ Not eat it at all

4 What lesson do the sisters need to learn?

- ○ They should wait until after dinner to eat cake.
- ○ Cake is not a good food for girls to eat.
- ○ They should keep secrets from each other.
- ○ Sharing is better than arguing.

GO

Birdhouse

Making a birdhouse is fun and easy. Remember, though, you will need some help with cutting.

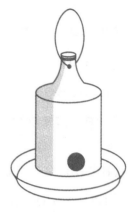

Use a large, empty, plastic bleach bottle or other large plastic bottle. Wash it out well. Punch two holes just below the lid. Tie a string through these holes. Leave a loop to hang the birdhouse.

Cut a hole near the bottom for the birds to enter. The hole should be about 2 inches wide. Different kinds of birds like holes of different sizes.

Glue a foil pie pan to the bottom of the bleach bottle. The birds can stand on this. Putting some seeds in the pan will attract birds to the house. When they see the opening, they will want to build a nest in it.

Hang your birdhouse in a nearby tree. Hang it high enough so cats will not be able to get to it.

5 The foil pie pan glued to the bottom is for —

○ the birds to stand on
○ hanging the birdhouse in the tree
○ keeping cats out of the birdhouse
○ the bird to build a nest

6 What will make the birdhouse best for a small bird?

○ Washing it out
○ A small hole
○ Lots of seed
○ A large hole

GO ➡

An Unusual Job

Mr. Johnson is a pet store owner. He has a job many people would like. He gets to take care of and play with lots of animals. He talks to people about what kind of pets they would like to have. He helps them learn to take care of their pets.

Not all pet store jobs are fun. Someone must clean the animals' cages. Their food must be put out every day. The water must be changed. Some of the pets must also be taken out for walks or allowed to <u>exercise</u>.

The pet store owner must have good reading and math skills. Mr. Johnson must read about new foods for the animals. He must know how to use numbers well when he runs his business.

The best part of his job is seeing a boy or girl get just the right pet. Mr. Johnson likes knowing that the child and the animal will soon be best friends.

 7 The part of his job that Mr. Johnson likes best is —

- ○ reading about new foods for the animals
- ○ helping each child get the right pet
- ○ cleaning the animals' cages
- ○ doing the math to run his business

 8 In this story, <u>exercise</u> is —

- ○ playing games like basketball
- ○ letting animals walk or run around
- ○ what Mr. Johnson likes to do after work
- ○ letting the pets rest

GO

Rainbows and Clouds

This is a special dessert that your family will enjoy. You will need three packages of colored gelatin mix, water, whipped topping, measuring cup, spoon, and a large plate.

Mix one package of gelatin. Heat one cup of water in the microwave for a minute. Stir in the gelatin powder. Mix well. Add one cup of cold water. Stir again. Pour this into the pan or dish. It will be a thin layer. Put it in the refrigerator for an hour or until it has set.

Mix the second package of gelatin the same way. Carefully pour it over the first layer in the dish. Let it chill for an hour or until it is set.

Mix the third package. Pour it over the other layers. Chill for an hour.

Cut the rainbow gelatin into squares. Carefully lift each square out of the dish. Set them on a plate. Add a "cloud" of whipped topping on one corner. This recipe makes several servings.

 9 After you mix the hot water, cold water, and gelatin powder, you should —

○ add more cold water
○ add the whipped topping
○ pour it into the pan or dish
○ cut it into squares

 10 A good time to make this dessert is —

○ in the morning before school
○ on a rainy Saturday afternoon
○ at night before going to bed
○ just before you leave on a trip

STOP

SAMPLE

428	100	8	4	2
	○	○	○	○

Listen carefully while you look at the item.

1

55	44	10	54
○	○	○	○

2

362	326	30062	36200
○	○	○	○

3

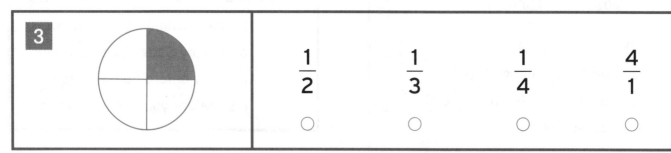

$\dfrac{1}{2}$ ○ $\dfrac{1}{3}$ ○ $\dfrac{1}{4}$ ○ $\dfrac{4}{1}$ ○

GO ➡

4

○   ○   ○   ○

5

$200 + 20$

202   20020   2200   220
○   ○   ○   ○

6

$4 - 3 = 1$ $4 + 3 = 7$
○   ○

$7 + 3 = 10$ $7 + 4 = 11$
○   ○

7

| 78 | | 112 |

93   71   131   60
○   ○   ○   ○

GO ➡

Magazines at Home

Rosa	📖 📖 📖 📖 📖 📖
Andy	📖 📖 📖 📖 📖 📖 📖 📖
Mark	📖 📖 📖
Holly	📖 📖 📖 📖
Lona	📖 📖 📖 📖 📖

8

| Rosa | Mark | Holly | Lona |
| ○ | ○ | ○ | ○ |

9

| 7 | 8 | 6 | 5 |
| ○ | ○ | ○ | ○ |

10

| Mark | Lona | Rosa | Holly |
| ○ | ○ | ○ | ○ |

GO ➡

11

847	801	719	730
○	○	○	○

12

$25 + 41 = 41 + \square$

66	16	41	25
○	○	○	○

13

○	○	○	○

14

SEPTEMBER

S	M	T	W	T	F	S
			1	2	3	4
5	6	7	8	9	10	11
12	13	14	15	16	17	18
19	20	21	22	22	24	25
26	27	28	29	30		

Sunday	Thursday
○	○
Tuesday	**Saturday**
○	○

STOP

SAMPLE

5 + ☐ = 5 | 10   5   0   ‑5
                  ○   ○   ○   ○

TIP After you mark your answer, get ready for the next question.

1

11   16   37   43
○   ○   ○   ○

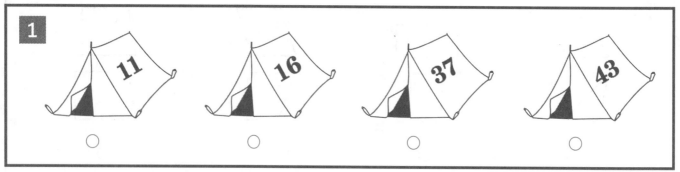

2

582   50082   5082   50802
○   ○   ○   ○

3

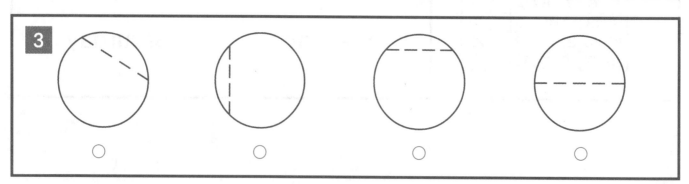

○   ○   ○   ○

GO ➡

4

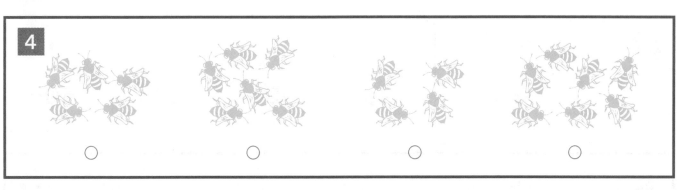

○　　　　　　○　　　　　　○　　　　　　○

5

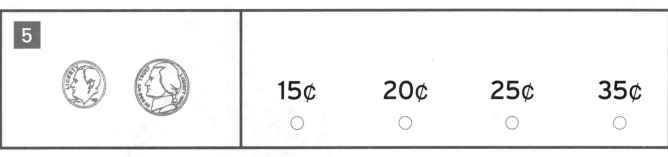

15¢　　　20¢　　　25¢　　　35¢

○　　　　○　　　　○　　　　○

6

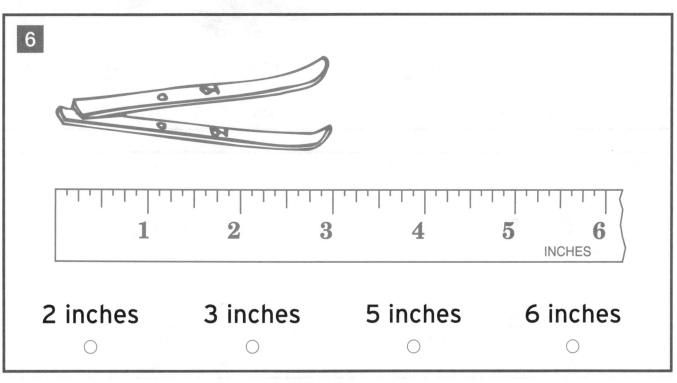

2 inches　　3 inches　　5 inches　　6 inches

○　　　　　○　　　　　○　　　　　○

7

| 2¢ | 10¢ | 20¢ | 50¢ |
| ○ | ○ | ○ | ○ |

8

15¢

| 2¢ | 10¢ | 12¢ | 15¢ |
| ○ | ○ | ○ | ○ |

9

$8 - 5 = \square$
○

$5 + 8 = \square$
○

$8 + 5 = \square$
○

$\square - 8 = 5$
○

GO ➡

10

624	453	296	375
○	○	○	○

11

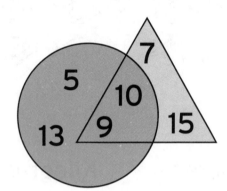

5	7	10	15
○	○	○	○

12

2:00	2:30	6:15	6:20
○	○	○	○

SAMPLE A

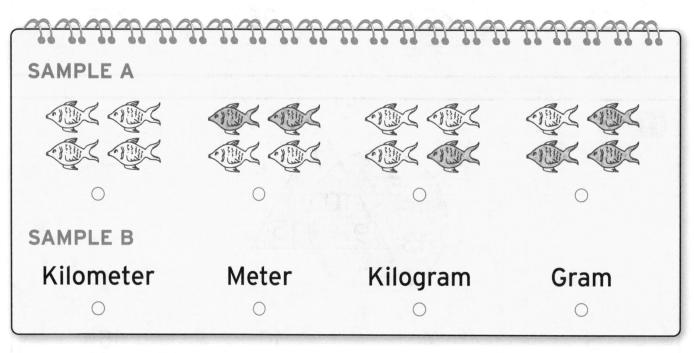

SAMPLE B

Kilometer	Meter	Kilogram	Gram
○	○	○	○

1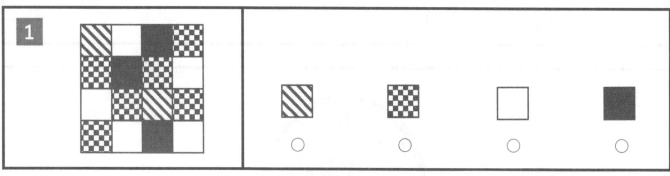

2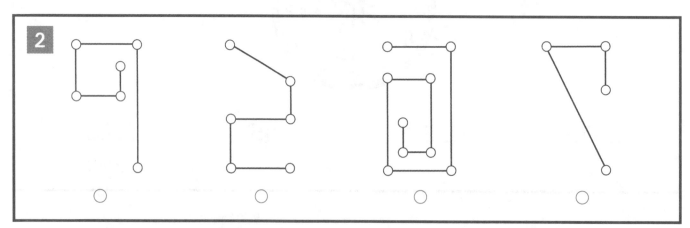

GO ➡

3

628	649	761	749
○	○	○	○

4

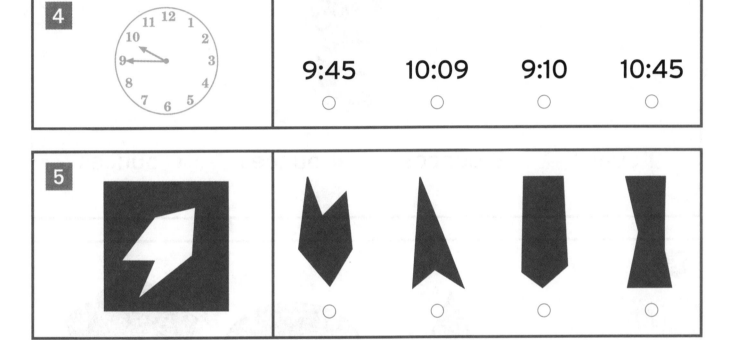

9:45	10:09	9:10	10:45
○	○	○	○

5

| | ○ | ○ | ○ | ○ |

6

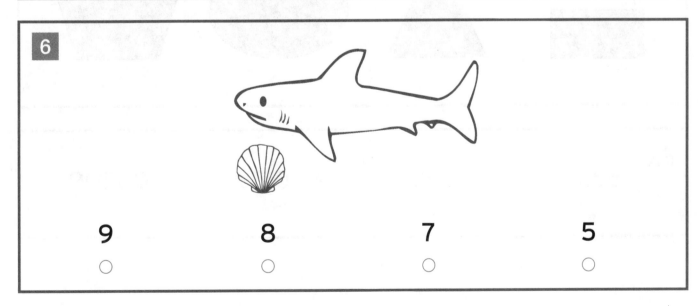

9	8	7	5
○	○	○	○

GO ➡

7

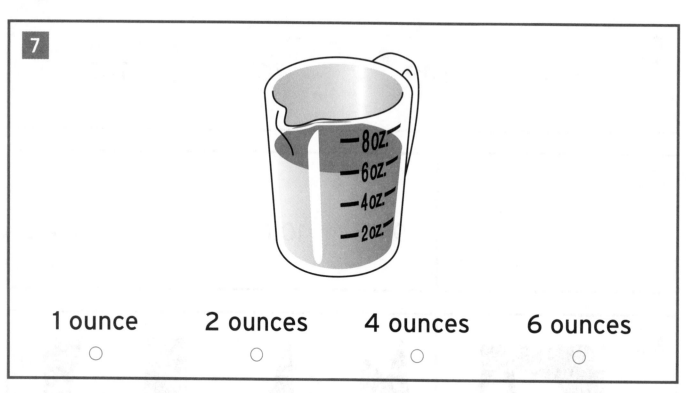

1 ounce ○   2 ounces ○   4 ounces ○   6 ounces ○

8

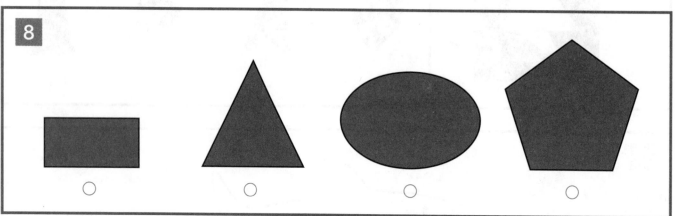

○   ○   ○   ○

9

639 ○   6039 ○   600139 ○   600309 ○

GO ➡

10

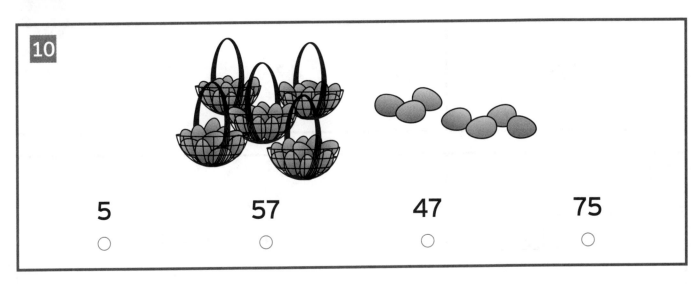

5	57	47	75
○	○	○	○

11

287	8	2	7	10
	○	○	○	○

12

200 + 70	2700	20070	270	2007
	○	○	○	○

13

80042	80402	800402	842
○	○	○	○

14

307	259	431	283
○	○	○	○

GO ➡

15

376

386	476	276	377
○	○	○	○

16

191		224

172	231	215	189
○	○	○	○

17

$2 + 7 = 9$
○

$5 - 3 = 2$
○

$5 + 2 = 7$
○

$7 - 4 = 3$
○

GO ➡

18

2×9

$9 - 2$ ○ $9 \div 2$ ○ $9 + 9$ ○ $2 + 9$ ○

19

$5 + \square = 6$

0 ○   1 ○   5 ○   10 ○

20

$45 + 21 = 21 + \square$

21 ○   24 ○   45 ○   66 ○

21

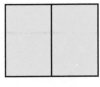   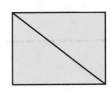   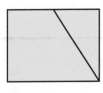   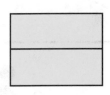

○   ○   ○   ○

STOP

SAMPLE A

5

2

10	7	3	2	NH
○	○	○	○	○

SAMPLE B

$$4 + 2 = \square$$

2	5	7	8	NH
○	○	○	○	○

Before you solve a problem, decide if you should add or subtract.

1

20

8

10	12	14	28	NH
○	○	○	○	○

GO ➡

2

13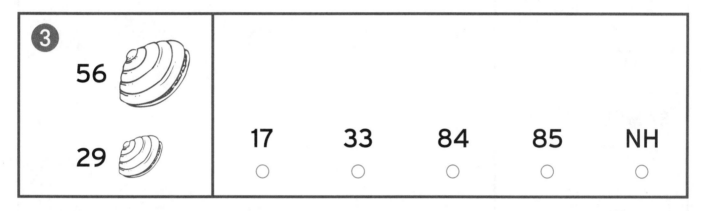

33

20	30	43	46	NH
○	○	○	○	○

3

56

29

17	33	84	85	NH
○	○	○	○	○

4

17

14

21	23	31	58	NH
○	○	○	○	○

5

$$7 + 4 = \square$$

11	12	14	47	NH
○	○	○	○	○

STOP

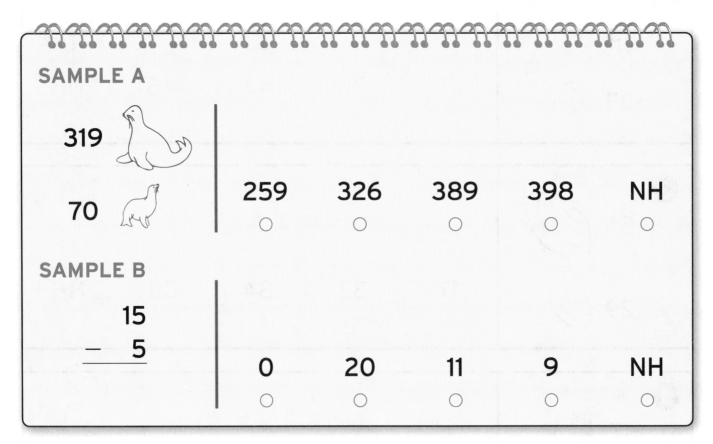

SAMPLE A

319

70

259	326	389	398	NH
○	○	○	○	○

SAMPLE B

15
− 5

0	20	11	9	NH
○	○	○	○	○

Stay with your first answer. Change it only if you are sure it is wrong.

1

53

17

70	46	44	36	NH
○	○	○	○	○

GO ➡

2

$$\square + 9 = 18$$

1	8	9	11	NH
○	○	○	○	○

3

$$\begin{array}{r} 37 \\ +7 \\ \hline \end{array}$$

30	41	45	47	NH
○	○	○	○	○

4

$$\begin{array}{r} 239 \\ -\,134 \\ \hline \end{array}$$

105	305	115	215	NH
○	○	○	○	○

5

$$80 - 50 = \square$$

130	50	40	30	NH
○	○	○	○	○

STOP

Unit 5

Test Yourself: Mathematics Procedures

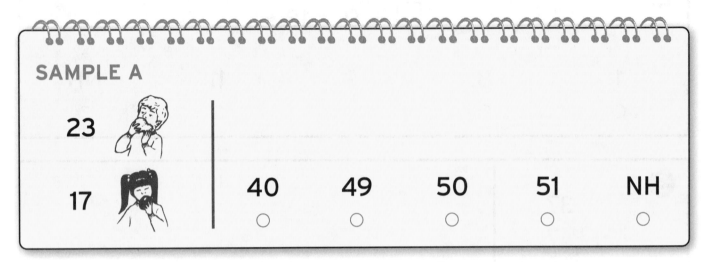

SAMPLE A

23

17

40	49	50	51	NH
○	○	○	○	○

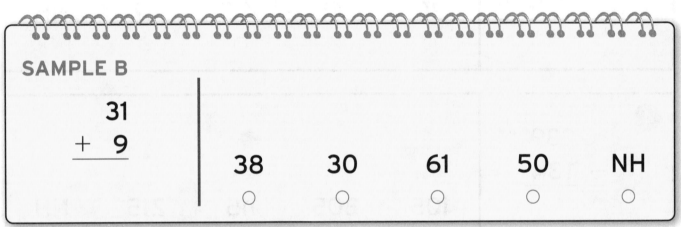

SAMPLE B

$$\begin{array}{r} 31 \\ +\ 9 \\ \hline \end{array}$$

38	30	61	50	NH
○	○	○	○	○

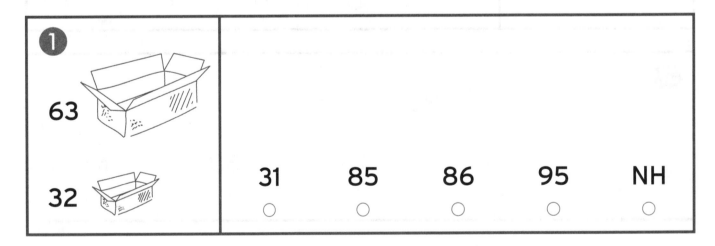

1

63

32

31	85	86	95	NH
○	○	○	○	○

GO ➡

2

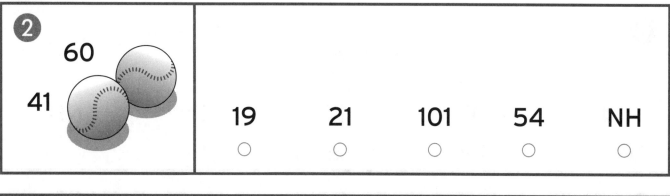

60

41

19   21   101   54   NH
○   ○   ○   ○   ○

3

82

24

60   62   98   106   NH
○   ○   ○   ○   ○

4

71

32

41   52   103   45   NH
○   ○   ○   ○   ○

5

29

55

86   32   76   85   NH
○   ○   ○   ○   ○

GO ➡

6

$$4 + 7 = \square$$

47   17   14   11   NH
○   ○   ○   ○   ○

7

916
+ 41

997   966   957   935   NH
○   ○   ○   ○   ○

8

88
− 22

110   66   56   78   NH
○   ○   ○   ○   ○

9

100
− 7

97   70   60   93   NH
○   ○   ○   ○   ○

SAMPLE A

<u>Toss</u> the <u>bal</u> <u>here</u>.

○   ○ ○

SAMPLE B

The <u>snow</u> <u>felt</u> very <u>coald</u>.

○   ○   ○

---

1 My sister <u>cride</u> when she <u>hurt</u> her <u>finger</u>.

○   ○   ○

---

2 Jake's <u>new</u> <u>shirt</u> is <u>bluue</u>

○ ○ ○

---

3 The <u>water</u> is not warm <u>enogh</u> for <u>swimming</u>.

○   ○   ○

---

4 May I have a <u>peece</u> of <u>apple</u> <u>pie</u>.

○   ○ ○

STOP

SAMPLE A

The <u>famly</u> <u>lived</u> in a big <u>house</u>.
○   ○   ○

SAMPLE B

We ate <u>birthday</u> <u>caik</u> at the <u>party</u>.
○   ○   ○

TIP

Say each underlined word to yourself while you look at it.

1   <u>Wish</u> your hands in the <u>bathroom</u> <u>sink</u>.
○   ○   ○

2   Blanca <u>went</u> to <u>camap</u> near a <u>lake</u>.
○   ○   ○

3   <u>Draw</u> a big <u>curcle</u> on the <u>board</u>.
○   ○   ○

4   I have an <u>extera</u> <u>pen</u> you can <u>borrow</u>.
○   ○   ○

STOP

SAMPLE A

Sam <u>gos</u> <u>home</u> for <u>lunch.</u>
   ◯   ◯   ◯

SAMPLE B

A <u>bird</u> was on the <u>barn</u> <u>rofe.</u>
◯   ◯ ◯

---

1   Let's <u>bake</u> <u>cookies</u> <u>soun.</u>
     ◯   ◯   ◯

2   I had a <u>dreem</u> <u>last</u> <u>night.</u>
      ◯   ◯   ◯

3   She <u>sat</u> <u>quietly</u> at her <u>dest.</u>
    ◯   ◯   ◯

4   <u>Meny</u> <u>men</u> like to <u>cook.</u>
  ◯   ◯   ◯

GO ➡

5 That <u>tree</u> has <u>rouph</u> <u>bark</u>.
    ○   ○   ○

6 <u>There</u> was <u>nowere</u> to <u>hide</u>.
    ○   ○   ○

7 She <u>nows</u> the <u>right</u> <u>answer</u>.
    ○   ○   ○

8 The <u>doctor</u> put a <u>kast</u> on Ken's <u>leg</u>.
    ○   ○   ○

9 The <u>babie</u> is <u>still</u> <u>asleep</u>.
    ○   ○   ○

10 We <u>kept</u> the <u>presnt</u> a <u>secret</u>.
    ○   ○   ○

STOP

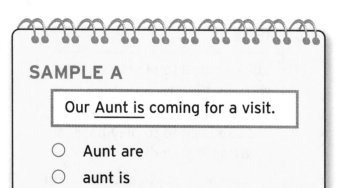

SAMPLE A

Our <u>Aunt is</u> coming for a visit.

- ○ Aunt are
- ○ aunt is
- ○ The way it is

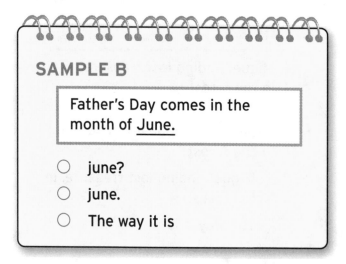

SAMPLE B

Father's Day comes in the month of <u>June.</u>

- ○ june?
- ○ june.
- ○ The way it is

Listen carefully while you look at the sentence and answer choices.

1 Do you know where my <u>book is!</u>

- ○ book is.
- ○ book is?
- ○ The way it is

3 The music <u>was</u> very loud.

- ○ are
- ○ were
- ○ The way it is

2 My cousin lives in <u>Austin Texas.</u>

- ○ Austin, Texas.
- ○ austin, texas.
- ○ The way it is

4 Our <u>teacher Mr. Santos</u> plays the piano.

- ○ Our teacher mr. Santos
- ○ Our teacher, Mr. Santos,
- ○ The way it is

STOP

SAMPLE C

Miguel finding lost treasure in the forest.

○ Miguel found lost treasure in the forest.

○ Miguel finding lost treasure. In the forest.

○ The way it is

SAMPLE D

Luke wanted to play baseball with his friends.

○ Luke wanted to play baseball. With his friends.

○ Luke wanting to play baseball with his friends.

○ The way it is

The group of words that sounds best is the right answer.

5 Black smoke come from the old truck.

○ Black smoke came from the old truck.

○ Black smoke came. From the old truck.

○ The way it is

7 The doctor looked. At the bump on Jamal's head.

○ The doctor looking at the bump on Jamal's head.

○ The doctor looked at the bump on Jamal's head.

○ The way it is

6 My sister is teaching me to play the piano.

○ My sister is teaching me. To play the piano.

○ My sister teach me to play the piano.

○ The way it is

STOP

SAMPLE E

> Terry is writing a story about how her family feeds birds. She wants to organize her ideas before she writes.

What should Terry do?

- ○ Buy a new pencil
- ○ Make an outline
- ○ Think of a funny story

SAMPLE F

> Eddie is writing a report about electricity. What should he do to get more ideas?

- ○ Read about electricity in an encyclopedia
- ○ Turn on a light in his house
- ○ Ask his friends if they have a flashlight

8 June is writing a story about her family's vacation.

Which idea should be first in her story?

- ○ Swimming in the ocean
- ○ Getting to the beach
- ○ Packing her suitcase

9 Matt is writing a letter to his grandmother telling her about his new puppy.

Which idea does <u>not</u> belong in Matt's letter?

- ○ The puppy's name
- ○ Why people like puppies
- ○ How big the puppy is

Listen carefully while you look at the answers.

STOP

Last summer, my family went on a camping trip. We slept in a big tent. One night, Mom heard a noise outside the tent. We all listened quietly. My Dad said it was a bear! The bear was looking for something to eat.

SAMPLE G

Which of these would go <u>best</u> after the last sentence?

○ I remember reading "Goldilocks and the Three Bears."

○ The bear went away when it found nothing to eat.

○ The tent was green and had a window in back.

Story 1

I like to visit my grandfather. Even when he is busy, my grandfather always plays with me. Once, he taught me how to play checkers. He wins all the time! At home, I practice playing checkers with Mom and Dad.

 10 Why was this story written?

○ To teach how to play checkers

○ To tell about a nice grandfather

○ To tell what games are fun to play

 11 Which of these would <u>not</u> go with this story?

○ It rained the last time we went to visit my grandfather.

○ Grandfather likes to take walks in the field with me.

○ I sometimes play checkers with my friends, too.

STOP

SAMPLE A

> My orange cat likes to sit in my lap.

- ○ lap?
- ○ lap!
- ○ The way it is

SAMPLE B

> Her big brother ran and caught the ball.

- ○ catch
- ○ catched
- ○ The way it is

Think about the question and then look carefully at the answer choices.

1 Our new house is at the end of Grand avenue.

- ○ Grand Avenue.
- ○ grand avenue.
- ○ The way it is

2 Jeremy taked a picture with his dad's camera.

- ○ are taking
- ○ took
- ○ The way it is

3 We run all the way home.

- ○ runned
- ○ ran
- ○ The way it is

4 At the beach my sister showed us that a clam live in the sand.

- ○ lives
- ○ are living
- ○ The way it is

STOP

SAMPLE C

> My pet turtle likes to eat. A lot of food.

- ○ My pet turtle like to eat a lot of food.
- ○ My pet turtle likes to eat a lot of food.
- ○ The way it is

SAMPLE D

> My sister wanted to play with her friends all day.

- ○ My sister wanted to play. With her friends all day.
- ○ My sister wanting to play with her friends all day.
- ○ The way it is

5

> While painting her picture. Meg dropped her brush.

- ○ While painting her picture, Meg dropped her brush.
- ○ While painting her picture, Meg dropping her brush.
- ○ The way it is

7

> John picked up his toys. And put them away.

- ○ John picked up his toys and put them away.
- ○ John picking up his toys and put them away.
- ○ The way it is

6

> In the blowing wind, the leafy branches shook.

- ○ In the blowing wind, the leafy branches shaking.
- ○ In the blowing wind. The leafy branches shook.
- ○ The way it is

8

> The cow walking across the field to the barn.

- ○ The cow walked across the field. To the barn.
- ○ The cow walked across the field to the barn.
- ○ The way it is

STOP

SAMPLE E

Mrs. Sanchez stirred a jar of water as she added sugar. When the sugar disappeared, she poured the sugar water into a red container. "What are you making?" asked Pablo. "This is food for hummingbirds," she answered. "Do you want to help me feed them?"

Which of these would go <u>best</u> after the last sentence?

○ Pablo smiled and said, "That would be fun!"

○ Mrs. Sanchez dried her hands on the towel.

○ Pablo went outside to play with his friends.

Story 1

Our school has a garden where we grow vegetables. Every student gets to plant one thing. I'm growing carrots. There is a prize for the biggest vegetable of each kind. I know my carrots will win a prize. No one else planted any!

 9 Why was this story written?

○ To make you eat more carrots

○ To show how to plant a garden

○ To tell about the school garden

 10 Which of these would <u>not</u> go with this story?

○ We eat the part of a carrot that is the root.

○ Many students grow corn because it is so tall.

○ The first prize is a blue ribbon.

GO

Story 2

Jenna and her family live near a warm beach. She had never seen snow except in pictures. During the winter break, Jenna went on vacation to the mountains. Jenna was going to see real snow. She was even going to learn to ski!

 11 Which of these would <u>not</u> go with this story?

- ○ Jenna loved the snow, but thought it was very cold.
- ○ Jenna likes other sports better than skiing.
- ○ Jenna had to borrow ski clothes from her friends.

 13 Which of these would go <u>best</u> after the last sentence?

- ○ It has to be cold to snow.
- ○ Jenna knew this trip would be wonderful.
- ○ Many people take their vacation during the summer.

 12 Why was this story written?

- ○ To tell about Jenna's vacation
- ○ To teach people how to ski
- ○ To show how warm the beach is

STOP

SAMPLE A

> Hurry, Antonio, don't let them catch <u>you</u>!

○ you

○ you?

○ The way it is

SAMPLE B

> Dad went to the <u>Store for a video.</u>

○ Store for a Video.

○ store for a video.

○ The way it is

1 At the library, we heard a story called <u>"cloud watch."</u>

○ "Cloud Watch."

○ "Cloud watch."

○ The way it is

4 After she sang, everyone <u>clapped</u> for a long time.

○ claps

○ clapping

○ The way it is

2 At the zoo, we all <u>seen</u> a baby tiger.

○ seeing

○ saw

○ The way it is

5 My grandparents will visit in <u>may.</u>

○ May?

○ May.

○ The way it is

3 Hi, Mark! Where have you <u>been!</u>

○ been?

○ been.

○ The way it is

GO ➡

61

6 For dinner, <u>Tom maked</u> some pizza.

○ Tom made
○ tom maked
○ The way it is

7 We live near the <u>Bay bridge.</u>

○ Bay Bridge?
○ Bay Bridge.
○ The way it is

8 They moved here from <u>Omaha Nebraska.</u>

○ Omaha, Nebraska.
○ omaha, nebraska.
○ The way it is

9 Can you guess how tall I <u>am?</u>

○ am!
○ am.
○ The way it is

10 She was very quiet <u>that Night.</u>

○ that Night?
○ that night.
○ The way it is

11 I saw a <u>Movie with Ellen.</u>

○ movie with Ellen.
○ Movie with ellen.
○ The way it is

12 I was eight when we <u>move</u> to Texas.

○ moved
○ is moving
○ The way it is

13 It rained last <u>week.</u>

○ week?
○ Week.
○ The way it is

STOP

SAMPLE C

A rooster crows every day at dawn.

○ A rooster crows. Every day at dawn.

○ A rooster crows every day. At dawn.

○ The way it is

SAMPLE D

Kittens drinking milk from a bowl on the floor.

○ Kittens drank milk. From a bowl on the floor.

○ Kittens drank milk from a bowl on the floor.

○ The way it is

 14 I am the oldest of four children.

○ I am the oldest. Of four children.

○ I being the oldest of four children.

○ The way it is

 16 Dirk took a nap. Because he was tired.

○ Dirk taking a nap because he was tired.

○ Dirk took a nap because he was tired.

○ The way it is

 15 After it got dark. We counted stars.

○ After it got dark we counted stars.

○ After it got dark we counting stars.

○ The way it is

 17 Lora poured some juice and drank it.

○ Lora pouring some juice and drinking it.

○ Lora poured some juice. And drank it.

○ The way it is

STOP

SAMPLES

My mom likes to swim, so we go to the pool once a week. Sometimes, when it's hot, she takes me every day. Mom taught me how to swim when I was only three. Swimming is my favorite sport now.

SAMPLE E

Why was this story written?

○ To tell how big the pool is
○ To explain how to swim
○ To tell about swimming

SAMPLE F

Which of these would go <u>best</u> after the last sentence?

○ It gets really hot in the summer.
○ I hope to be in the Olympics someday.
○ Sometimes the water is cold at first.

GO ➡

Story 1

Yesterday was a special day at our house. We took my little brother to the library. He was getting his first library card, and he was very excited. It took him a long time to pick out a book.

 18 Which of these would go <u>best</u> after the last sentence?

○ The name of his book is "Mr. Fish Runs the School."

○ Our library is a big building all the way downtown.

○ Sometimes we get to take out videos at the library, too.

 19 Which of these does <u>not</u> go with the story?

○ My brother just learned to read.

○ You must return books to the library.

○ He asked me to help him read the book.

GO

Story 2

My family went on a trip to a nature museum. We saw shells, rocks, and insects. The best part of the museum was underwater! Through a window, we saw fish coming out of their eggs. Sometimes they got stuck in the rocks.

 20 Which of these would go <u>best</u> after the last sentence?

○ They had to wiggle to get loose.
○ We didn't get to see any ducks.
○ I once saw a chicken egg hatch.

 21 Why was this story written?

○ To tell where fish come from
○ To explain about shells and rocks
○ To tell about a special trip

 22 Which of these would <u>not</u> go with this story?

○ My parents like to take us to museums.
○ Fishing is my favorite hobby.
○ Some of the insects were really strange.

GO ➡

Story 3

Carly likes building sand castles at the beach. She spends most of her summer days building with sand. Small boxes and cups help shape the sand into castle walls. An old spoon is perfect for digging paths, tunnels, and doorways.

 23 Which of these would go <u>best</u> at the end of this story?

- ○ Sand castle building is done all over the world.
- ○ Summer vacation lasts from June to September.
- ○ Carly hopes to win a sand castle contest someday.

 25 Why was this story written?

- ○ To tell about living in a castle
- ○ To tell what old castles are made of
- ○ To tell what Carly does in the summer

 24 Which of these does <u>not</u> belong in this story?

- ○ Carly's parents once visited a real castle.
- ○ People stop to stare at Carly's sand castles.
- ○ Carly's sand castles are over two feet tall.

GO ➡

Story 4

Today, we learned how to paint a sunset. First, we took a sponge and made our paper very wet. Across the middle, we painted yellow and red stripes. Then, we painted dark blue across the top. Finally, we used the wet sponge to blend the stripes together.

 26 | Why was this story written?

○ To tell how to paint a sunset

○ To describe a sunset

○ To teach about all the colors

 27 | Which of these would go <u>best</u> after the last sentence?

○ Sometimes, after a rainstorm, a sunset looks very pretty.

○ When our pictures were dry, we painted trees on them.

○ I like to paint almost as much as I like to read.

 28 | Which of these would <u>not</u> go with this story?

○ The teacher put our paintings on the wall for our parents to see.

○ The red and yellow made orange when they mixed together.

○ At home, I have a box of crayons that I use for my drawings.

 STOP

Unit 8 Listening
Lesson 8a **Listening Skills**

SAMPLE A

- ○ listen
- ○ act
- ○ argue

SAMPLE B

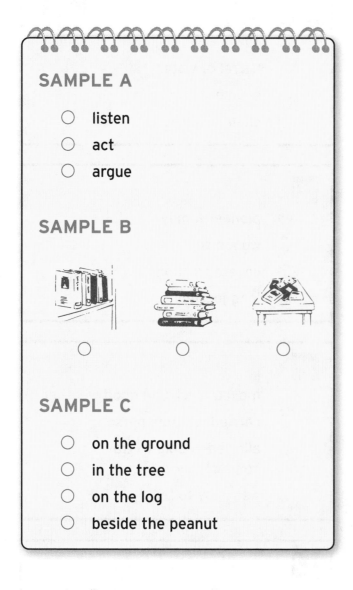

- ○   ○   ○

SAMPLE C

- ○ on the ground
- ○ in the tree
- ○ on the log
- ○ beside the peanut

Listen carefully while you look at the words or pictures.

1
- ○ get lost
- ○ get hurt
- ○ trip

2
- ○ smart
- ○ wrong
- ○ fast

3
- ○ shout
- ○ laugh
- ○ cry

4
- ○ wrap around
- ○ weave
- ○ carry

GO ➡

5
- ○ collect
- ○ throw
- ○ see

6
- ○ wait
- ○ listen
- ○ rush

7

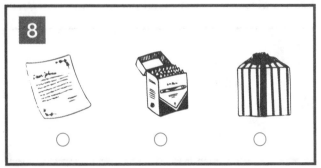

- ○   ○   ○

8

- ○   ○   ○

9
- ○ cow
- ○ barrel of water
- ○ saddle
- ○ chair

10
- ○ pioneer family
- ○ wagon train
- ○ covered wagon
- ○ long journey

11
- ○ moved quickly in good weather
- ○ carried just one person
- ○ allowed people to travel comfortably
- ○ was easy to build

12
- ○ a small table
- ○ dress-up clothes
- ○ a sack of canned food
- ○ the family's dishes

STOP

SAMPLE A

- ○ divide into pieces
- ○ plant
- ○ eat quickly

SAMPLE B

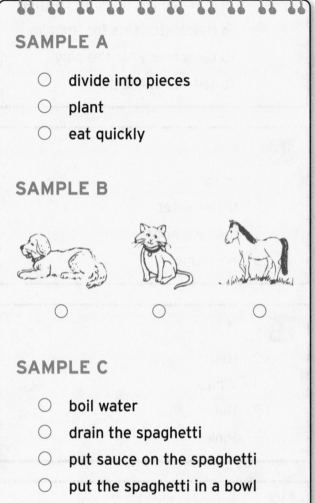

○   ○   ○

SAMPLE C

- ○ boil water
- ○ drain the spaghetti
- ○ put sauce on the spaghetti
- ○ put the spaghetti in a bowl

TIP

If you aren't sure which answer is correct, take your best guess.

1
- ○ first
- ○ next
- ○ last

2
- ○ small plant
- ○ bird
- ○ worm

3
- ○ cold
- ○ wet
- ○ dry

4
- ○ grew
- ○ escaped
- ○ repeated

GO ➡

5

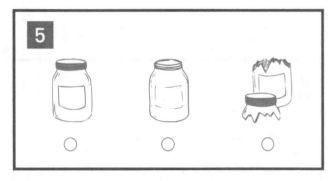

○   ○   ○

6

○   ○   ○

7

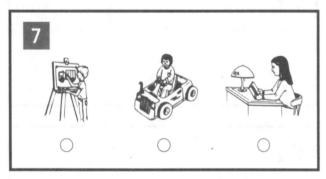

○   ○   ○

8

○   ○   ○

9

○   To practice her lines for the play
○   To thank students for the play
○   To be scenery for the play
○   To tell about the play

10

○   in the clouds
○   underwater
○   inside a house
○   on a ship

11

○   Red
○   White
○   Black
○   Pink

12

○   Betsy
○   Frank
○   Peter
○   Oliver

STOP

Test Yourself: Listening

SAMPLE A

- ○ rest
- ○ prize
- ○ drink

SAMPLE B

- ○ cross it
- ○ find it
- ○ make it

1

- ○ shout
- ○ jump
- ○ stand

2

- ○ dirty
- ○ cracked
- ○ missing

3

- ○ interesting
- ○ friendly
- ○ quiet

4

- ○ keep
- ○ share
- ○ pass

5

- ○ wash
- ○ paint
- ○ cut

6

- ○ funny
- ○ helpful
- ○ surprising

GO ➡

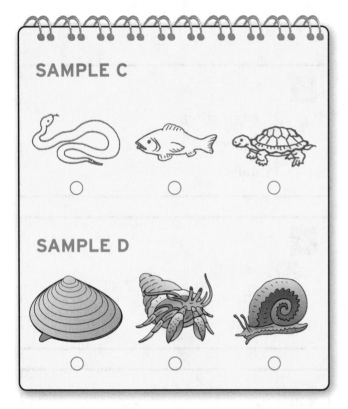

SAMPLE C

SAMPLE D

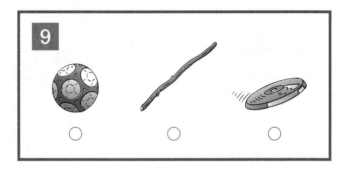

9

10

7

11

8

GO

SAMPLE E

- ○ It had fingerprints on it.
- ○ His mom asked him to.
- ○ He wanted to make money.
- ○ It made the baby giggle.

SAMPLE F

- ○ Made faces
- ○ Told jokes
- ○ Did a dance
- ○ Went and hid

12
- ○ "Kelly Tells How"
- ○ "Staying at Kelly's"
- ○ "Cooking with Kelly"
- ○ "Nora's Best Friend"

13
- ○ cooking
- ○ planting
- ○ shopping
- ○ playing

14
- ○ Lying in the sun
- ○ Making the dirt soft
- ○ Digging a small hole
- ○ Buying the plants

15
- ○ wear gloves
- ○ use a bowl
- ○ plant in rows
- ○ own a shovel

16
- ○ They look pretty.
- ○ They taste good.
- ○ They make nice gifts.
- ○ They smell good.

17
- ○ shy
- ○ smart
- ○ kind
- ○ strong

GO ➡

18
- ○ watched her classmates
- ○ asked a question
- ○ checked the spelling
- ○ turned bright pink

19
- ○ She sat at the teacher's desk.
- ○ She got to leave the classroom.
- ○ The new girl was friendly.
- ○ The teacher said nice things.

20
- ○ helpful
- ○ careful
- ○ whiny
- ○ proud

21
- ○ Knead the bread
- ○ Clean the kitchen
- ○ Make some cookies
- ○ Bake the bread

22
- ○ "Summer Sundays"
- ○ "A Fine Family Dinner"
- ○ "Baking and Being Together"
- ○ "Too Many Cooks in the Kitchen"

23
- ○ Measured the flour
- ○ Got out the loaf pans
- ○ Turned on the oven
- ○ The paragraph does not say.

24
- ○ impatient with people
- ○ an experienced baker
- ○ rarely around Kevin
- ○ a professional cook

25
- ○ confused
- ○ hopeful
- ○ restless
- ○ pleased

STOP

SAMPLE A

rewrite	fallen	popcorn
○	○	○

SAMPLE B

stops	stopped	stopping
○	○	○

1

sadness	catfish	thankful
○	○	○

2

lighthouse	remember	umbrella
○	○	○

3

beautiful	newspaper	together
○	○	○

4

exploring	business	playground
○	○	○

5

running	runs	runner
○	○	○

6

nearer	nearly	nearest
○	○	○

7

pulling	pulled	pulls
○	○	○

8

wanted	wants	wanting
○	○	○

STOP

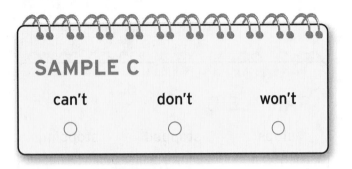

SAMPLE C

can't	don't	won't
○	○	○

SAMPLE D

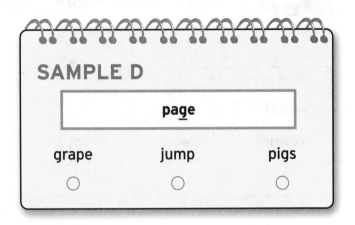

page

grape	jump	pigs
○	○	○

9

how's	who's	there's
○	○	○

10

he'd	he's	he'll
○	○	○

11

they're	you're	we're
○	○	○

12

I'll	we'll	she'll
○	○	○

13

end

read	best	dine
○	○	○

14

take

file	knit	cool
○	○	○

15

cloth

hot	thin	heat
○	○	○

16

bold

child	band	doll
○	○	○

GO

17 <u>n</u>ose

mole   head   knee

○   ○   ○

18 <u>b</u><u>oo</u>t

top   soup   cook

○   ○   ○

19 t<u>oy</u>

point   floppy   stone

○   ○   ○

20 h<u>o</u>pe

how   pop   load

○   ○   ○

21 <u>sh</u>oe

sock   each   rush

○   ○   ○

22 s<u>low</u>

lose   boat   wood

○   ○   ○

23 <u>g</u>row

angry   tiger   biggest

○   ○   ○

24 <u>wh</u>eel

hole   chew   why

○   ○   ○

25 <u>l</u>oud

flower   good   lost

○   ○   ○

26 bri<u>ng</u>

danger   long   grin

○   ○   ○

GO ➡

27 leap

| pale | seek | learn |
| ○ | ○ | ○ |

28 c**a**p

| place | call | back |
| ○ | ○ | ○ |

29 stee**r**

| step | farm | deed |
| ○ | ○ | ○ |

30 **ch**air

| stay | bench | class |
| ○ | ○ | ○ |

31 **n**ine

| sky | nail | kitten |
| ○ | ○ | ○ |

32 **str**eet

| stand | strike | treat |
| ○ | ○ | ○ |

33 **f**irst

| ring | fair | burn |
| ○ | ○ | ○ |

34 **r**are

| pair | rack | real |
| ○ | ○ | ○ |

35 m**u**le

| lump | zoom | come |
| ○ | ○ | ○ |

36 m**a**ke

| rail | add | coat |
| ○ | ○ | ○ |

37 c**r**oss

| soon | rock | post |
| ○ | ○ | ○ |

STOP

SAMPLE A

A <u>feast</u> is a kind of —

- ○ party
- ○ fight
- ○ meal
- ○ animal

SAMPLE B

To <u>tell</u> is to —

- ○ find
- ○ hope
- ○ say
- ○ ask

1 To <u>trust</u> is to —

- ○ pass
- ○ believe
- ○ help
- ○ ignore

3 To <u>punch</u> is to —

- ○ stop
- ○ hit
- ○ shut
- ○ run

2 <u>Happy</u> means —

- ○ real
- ○ pretty
- ○ new
- ○ glad

4 A building that is <u>high</u> is —

- ○ tall
- ○ old
- ○ brick
- ○ thin

GO ➡

5 To <u>repair</u> means to —

- ○ cut
- ○ pay
- ○ fix
- ○ slip

6 To <u>speak</u> is to —

- ○ plan
- ○ show
- ○ wave
- ○ talk

7 A <u>sack</u> is a kind of —

- ○ tool
- ○ bag
- ○ shelf
- ○ box

8 To <u>grab</u> something is to —

- ○ turn it
- ○ spend it
- ○ take it
- ○ spill it

9 <u>Everything</u> means —

- ○ all
- ○ most
- ○ some
- ○ none

10 A place that is <u>calm</u> is —

- ○ green
- ○ wide
- ○ open
- ○ quiet

STOP

SAMPLE C

Try not to <u>miss</u> the basket.

In which sentence does the word <u>miss</u> mean the same thing as in the sentence above?

- ○ Did you <u>miss</u> me yesterday?
- ○ Don't <u>miss</u> this movie.
- ○ He might <u>miss</u> the target.
- ○ I <u>miss</u> my cousins in Texas.

 The campers <u>saw</u> a raccoon.

In which sentence does the word <u>saw</u> mean the same thing as in the sentence above?

- ○ The worker got a new <u>saw</u>.
- ○ The owner <u>saw</u> me to the door.
- ○ We <u>saw</u> the movie last week.
- ○ They will <u>saw</u> down the tree.

 The circus show was in a <u>ring</u>.

In which sentence does the word <u>ring</u> mean the same thing as in the sentence above?

- ○ Put this <u>ring</u> on your finger.
- ○ We heard a telephone <u>ring</u>.
- ○ Horses ran around the <u>ring</u>.
- ○ The tub had a <u>ring</u> of dirt.

 The teacher wants us to <u>change</u> seats.

In which sentence does the word <u>change</u> mean the same thing as in the sentence above?

- ○ We kept our <u>change</u> in a big jar.
- ○ Let's <u>change</u> into warm clothes.
- ○ A seed will <u>change</u> into a flower.
- ○ Will you <u>change</u> places with me?

STOP

SAMPLE D

> Those girls look <u>similar</u> because they are sisters. <u>Similar</u> means —

- ○ smart
- ○ alike
- ○ small
- ○ tidy

SAMPLE E

> We didn't want to stand for the whole game, so we found a good spot in the <u>bleachers</u>. <u>Bleachers</u> are —

- ○ benches
- ○ crowds
- ○ fields
- ○ halls

14 He pretended to be nice, but he was really <u>cruel</u>. <u>Cruel</u> means —

- ○ unusual
- ○ busy
- ○ unkind
- ○ dull

16 Everyone liked Hector because he was an <u>agreeable</u> boy. <u>Agreeable</u> means —

- ○ proud
- ○ lost
- ○ silly
- ○ nice

15 Her happy face turned <u>sorrowful</u> when she found out the team had lost. <u>Sorrowful</u> means —

- ○ cute
- ○ sad
- ○ tired
- ○ old

17 The pioneer family was warm and safe inside their log <u>shelter</u>. A <u>shelter</u> is a —

- ○ fire
- ○ wagon
- ○ home
- ○ tool

STOP

Test Practice

Unit 9

Test 3 **Reading Comprehension**

Going to School

Joy was walking to school in the morning. She was a little late. "I must hurry," said Joy. Then a car stopped and a door opened. It was Joy's best friend Tina asking if she wanted a ride. Joy said yes and hopped inside.

SAMPLE A

Where does this story take place?

- ○ At a house
- ○ On a street
- ○ At a school
- ○ In a parking lot

SAMPLE B

The boxes show some things that happened in the story.

| Joy was walking to school. | → | | → | Joy hopped inside the car. |

Which of these belongs in the empty box?

- ○ The school bell rang.
- ○ Joy asked for a ride.
- ○ A door opened.
- ○ Joy said she was late.

GO ➡

Park Rules

Help make our park a safe, clean place for everyone. We ask visitors to follow six simple rules:

1. Put all trash in garbage cans.

2. Keep pets on leashes.

3. Clean up after your pets.

4. Ride bikes only on the bike paths.

5. Children should be accompanied by an adult.

6. Do not leave food on the picnic tables. It attracts wild animals.

1 These rules tell how to —

- ◯ find a place
- ◯ win a game
- ◯ keep a place safe
- ◯ play a simple game

2 You will need rule 6 if you —

- ◯ are with a child
- ◯ ride a bike
- ◯ have a picnic
- ◯ have a pet

3 You do <u>not</u> need rules 2 and 3 if you —

- ◯ walk your pet without a leash
- ◯ leave your pet at home
- ◯ feed your pet picnic scraps
- ◯ keep your pet away from children

GO ➡

Earth Day

I like holidays. They are special days. Today is my favorite holiday. It is called Earth Day. It is a day to celebrate the Earth. People all over the world celebrate Earth Day. They do different things. They sing, dance, and hold parades. My family hikes on Earth Day. We pack a lunch and pick a trail. We hike all day. Everywhere we look we see the Earth's beauty. We celebrate the Earth's beauty on Earth Day.

4 This story was written <u>mainly</u> to —

- ○ show how to do something
- ○ tell what a family does on one day
- ○ get you to try something new
- ○ tell what a special place looks like

5 This family celebrates Earth Day with a —

- ○ game
- ○ dance
- ○ hike
- ○ parade

Salad Pizza

"What is this?" asked Hannah. She pointed to a spinach plant in Grandma's garden.

"It goes in a salad," said Grandma.

"I love salad!" said Hannah.

"I know," said Grandma. "Let's pick some." Hannah and Grandma picked a little spinach. They put it in their basket.

"Are those for a salad, too?" asked Hannah. This time she pointed at some chives.

"Yes," said Grandma. "These are skinny onions. Smell them." Hannah put her face in the chives. She took a big sniff.

"Mmm," said Hannah. "They smell good."

Grandma and Hannah washed their basket of vegetables under the hose. After that, they went inside to make lunch.

Hannah stood on a short stool. Grandma rolled out a ball of white dough. Hanna was puzzled. What kind of salad had dough? Grandma put red tomato sauce on the dough. Then she chopped the spinach and the chives. She sprinkled them on top. Last, she added cheese. Grandma put the salad in the oven. Now Hannah was really surprised.

"Grandma?" asked Hannah. "Why are you baking our salad?"

Grandma wiped her hands on her apron and laughed. She could see why Hannah was confused.

"Our salad needs to be baked because it is part salad and part pizza," said Grandma.

6 In this story, the basket is for —

- ○ flowers
- ○ vegetables
- ○ muffins
- ○ fruit

7 What did Hannah pick first?

- ○ spinach
- ○ onions
- ○ tomatoes
- ○ lettuce

8 What will Grandma and Hannah probably do next?

- ○ put the pizza in the oven
- ○ go into the garden
- ○ set the table for lunch
- ○ make a big green salad

9 The boxes show some things that happened in the story.

| Grandma rolled out the dough. | → | | → | Grandma chopped the spinach and chives. |

Which of these belongs in the empty box?

- ○ Grandma sprinkled cheese on.
- ○ Grandma put tomato sauce on.
- ○ Grandma wiped her hands.
- ○ Grandma put it in the oven.

10 What did Hannah learn in this story?

- ○ Things that grow in gardens taste funny.
- ○ Making pizza dough is simple.
- ○ Caring for a garden is hard work.
- ○ Things that go in salads go on pizzas, too.

GO ➡

The Missing Seeds

"Oh, dear, oh dear," said Squirrel. "Where did I put those seeds?"

He looked everywhere. They weren't in the tree trunk. They weren't under the stone. They weren't by the fence. <u>Where were they?</u>

"What are you looking for, Son?" Pappa asked.

"My sunflower seeds!" cried Squirrel. "I hid them here last month, but now I can't find them." Squirrel's eyes filled with tears. He thought Pappa would give him a scolding.

But Pappa wanted to help. "Try looking over there," he said. Pappa pointed to a patch of tall yellow flowers. They were the tallest flowers Squirrel had ever seen.

"I did not hide my seeds in a patch of flowers," said Squirrel. Still, he went to look. Suddenly, Squirrel's nose began to twitch. He smelled sunflower seeds. Then he started to dig.

GO ➡️

11 Where did Squirrel look for the seeds?

○ In a hole

○ In a bush

○ In a nest

○ In a tree

13 At the end of the story, Squirrel did not know that —

○ he could smell sunflower seeds

○ his Pappa wanted to help him

○ he hid the seeds a month ago

○ his seeds had become flowers

12 When Squirrel told Pappa what he was looking for, he felt —

○ angry

○ excited

○ worried

○ hopeful

14 What will probably happen next?

○ Pappa will get angry with Squirrel.

○ Squirrel will keep looking for his seeds.

○ Pappa will go find his own seeds.

○ Squirrel will tell Pappa to go away.

GO ➡

Cheesy Noodles Contest

For Children Ages 5-10

How to Enter:

1. Buy a box of Cheesy Noodles.

2. Have a parent, grandparent, or other adult cook the Cheesy Noodles so you can taste them.

3. Write a song about Cheesy Noodles. Your song must be at least six lines long. It should tell why you like to eat Cheesy Noodles.

4. Send your song and the empty box of Cheesy Noodles to:

   Cheesy Noodles Company
   333 Tillamook Street
   Aberdeen, Wisconsin 53706

5. Be sure to send a stamped envelope with your name and address on it. We will send you information about the contest winners.

NOTE: Your song must be mailed <u>before</u> September 9. Winners will be flown by airplane to Wisconsin. They will get to be in a television ad for Cheesy Noodles. They will also win a free case of Cheesy Noodles.

---

15 To enter the contest, you should first —

- ○ write a song
- ○ talk to people
- ○ buy something
- ○ write a letter

16 To win the contest, your song must have at least —

- ○ 4 lines
- ○ 6 lines
- ○ 8 lines
- ○ 10 lines

STOP

SAMPLE A

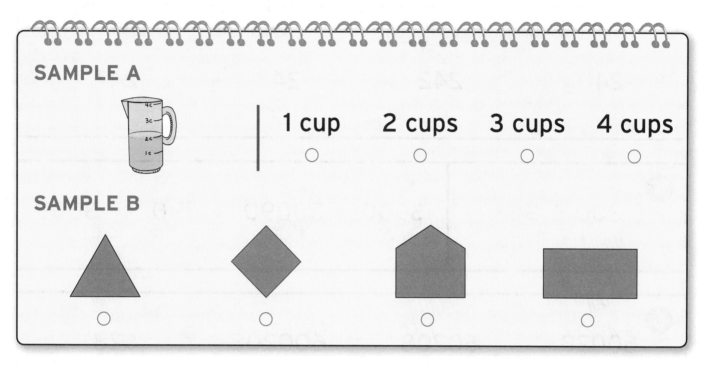

1 cup	2 cups	3 cups	4 cups
○	○	○	○

SAMPLE B

○   ○   ○   ○

1

○   ○   ○ ○

2
900602	9062	90062	962
○	○	○	○

GO ➡

3

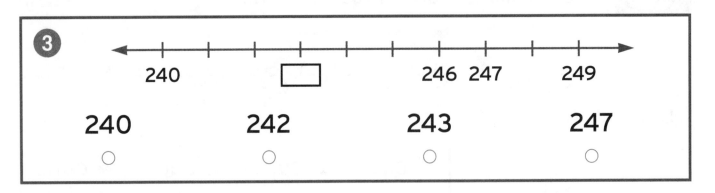

240   242   243   247
○   ○   ○   ○

4

$300 + 90$

3900   30090   390   3009
○   ○   ○   ○

5

60028   60208   600208   628
○   ○   ○   ○

6

835, 782, 904, 769
○

769, 782, 835, 904
○

782, 769, 835, 904
○

904, 769, 782, 835
○

7

539

529   439   639   538
○   ○   ○   ○

GO ➡

8

7 − 4 = 3   3 + 3 = 6   7 + 4 = 11   3 + 1 = 4

○   ○   ○   ○

9

5 × 2 | 5 − 2   5 ÷ 2   5 + 5   2 + 5

○   ○   ○   ○

10

☐ + 7 = 7 | 14   7   1   0

○   ○   ○   ○

11

23 + 36 = 36 + ☐ | 23   13   36   59

○   ○   ○   ○

12

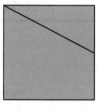 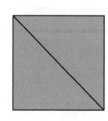 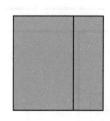 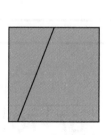

○   ○   ○   ○

GO ➡

13

$\dfrac{1}{2}$ ○ $\dfrac{1}{3}$ ○ $\dfrac{1}{4}$ ○ $\dfrac{3}{1}$ ○

14   126 127 128

○   ○ ○   ○

15

35   37   41

40 ○   39 ○   43 ○   38 ○

16

4 ○   5 ○   10 ○   11 ○

17

| 64 | 67 | 70 | | 76 |

71 ○   74 ○   73 ○   72 ○

GO ➡

18-19

Cans Collected by Ms. Nelson's Class

Monday	🥫🥫🥫🥫🥫🥫
Tuesday	🥫🥫🥫🥫🥫🥫🥫🥫🥫🥫🥫
Wednesday	🥫🥫🥫🥫🥫🥫🥫🥫🥫
Thursday	🥫🥫🥫🥫🥫🥫🥫🥫🥫🥫🥫🥫
Friday	🥫🥫🥫🥫🥫🥫🥫🥫🥫

18

Tuesday	Wednesday	Thursday	Friday
○	○	○	○

19

11	9	20	19
○	○	○	○

20

Favorite Sport

Baseball	10
Soccer	8
Football	7
Basketball	12

12	8	4	3
○	○	○	○

GO ➡

21

Cinderella	⊞⊞
Jack and the Beanstalk	⊞⊞ IIII
Goldilocks	IIII
The Three Little Pigs	⊞⊞ III

- ○ *Cinderella*
- ○ *Jack and the Beanstalk*
- ○ *Goldilocks*
- ○ *The Three Little Pigs*

22

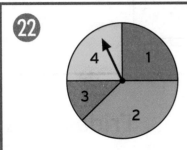

| 1 | 2 | 3 | 4 |
| ○ | ○ | ○ | ○ |

23

24

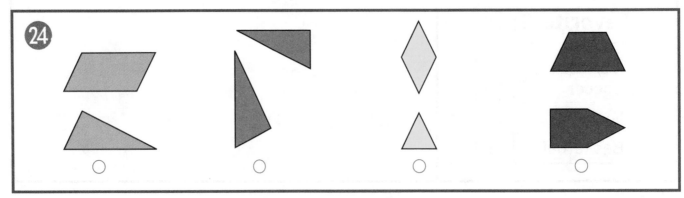

GO ➡

25

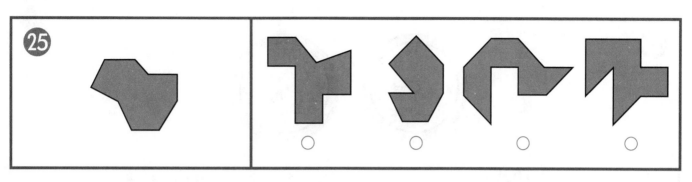

26

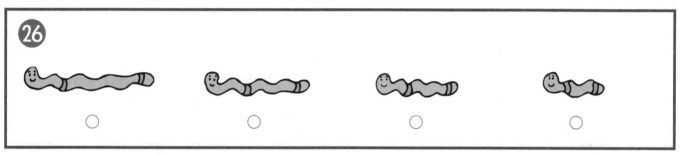

27

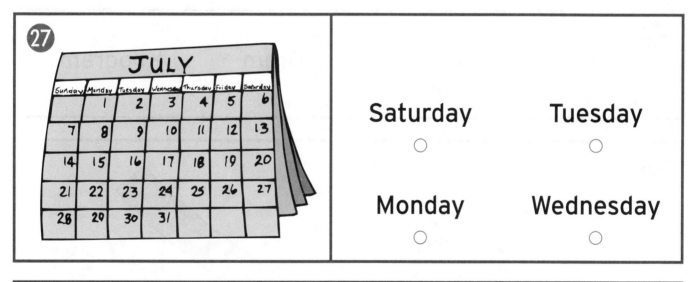

Saturday   Tuesday
   ○   ○

Monday   Wednesday
   ○   ○

28

9:25   4:15   4:30   4:45
  ○   ○   ○   ○

GO ➡

29

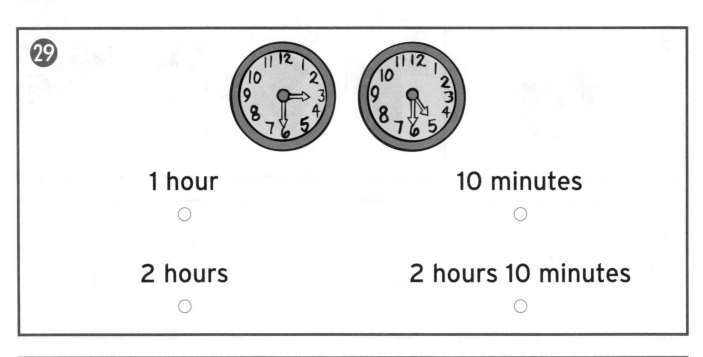

1 hour
○

10 minutes
○

2 hours
○

2 hours 10 minutes
○

30

Meter
○

Liter
○

Gram
○

Kilogram
○

31

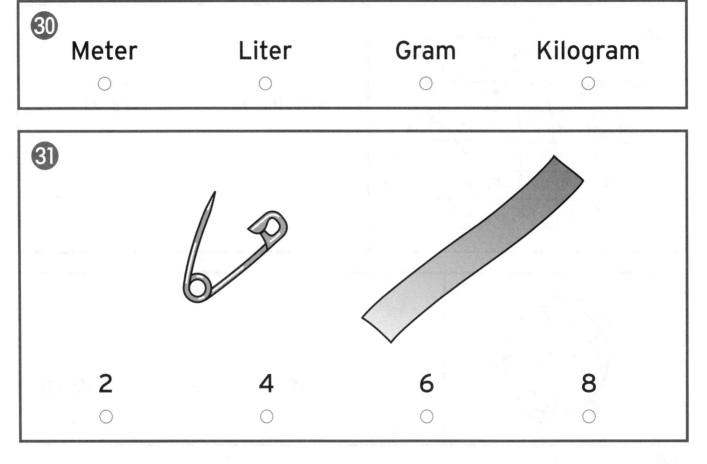

2
○

4
○

6
○

8
○

STOP

SAMPLE A

3   5

6	7	8	9	NH
○	○	○	○	○

SAMPLE B

$$7 - 3 = \square$$

2	3	10	11	NH
○	○	○	○	○

1

6   9

3	10	14	15	NH
○	○	○	○	○

GO ➡

2

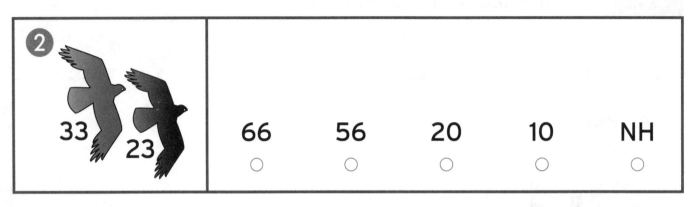

33 23

66	56	20	10	NH
○	○	○	○	○

3

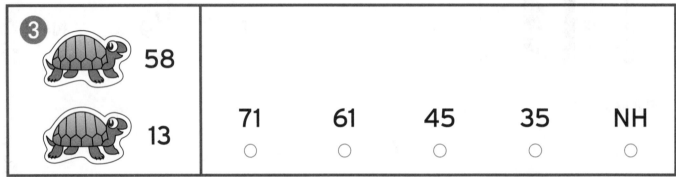

58

13

71	61	45	35	NH
○	○	○	○	○

4

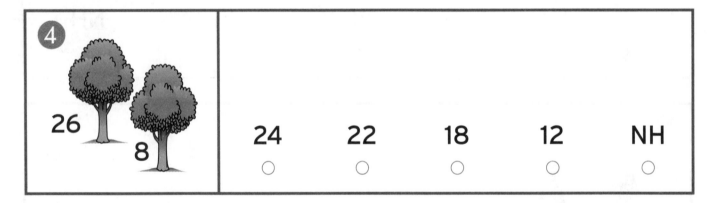

26 8

24	22	18	12	NH
○	○	○	○	○

5

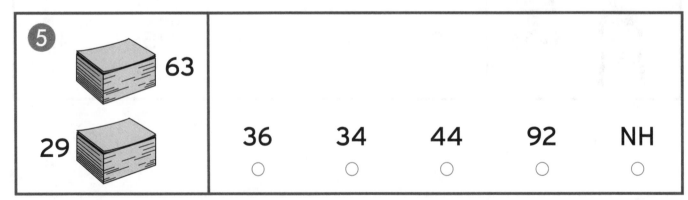

63

29

36	34	44	92	NH
○	○	○	○	○

GO ➡

6

$$\square + 5 = 14$$

8	9	10	19	NH
○	○	○	○	○

7

$$4 + 2 + 9 = \square$$

17	16	15	14	NH
○	○	○	○	○

8

$$\begin{array}{r} 25 \\ 12 \\ + 16 \\ \hline \end{array}$$

28	43	48	53	NH
○	○	○	○	○

9

$$\begin{array}{r} 84 \\ + 7 \\ \hline \end{array}$$

81	83	91	811	NH
○	○	○	○	○

GO ➡

10

$$673 - 23$$

550	553	640	650	NH
○	○	○	○	○

11

$$50 - 6$$

56	54	46	44	NH
○	○	○	○	○

12

$$543 - 341$$

102	192	202	884	NH
○	○	○	○	○

13

$$80 - 50$$

40	30	20	10	NH
○	○	○	○	○

STOP

SAMPLE A

My cat <u>ate</u> the <u>whule</u> can of <u>food</u>.
   ○   ○   ○

SAMPLE B

You can have a <u>bol</u> of <u>soup</u> for <u>lunch</u>.
     ○   ○   ○

---

1   Tina <u>swimms</u> at the <u>pool</u> in the <u>park</u>.
   ○   ○   ○

---

2   I like to <u>laugh</u> at <u>funny</u> <u>joakes</u>.
    ○   ○ ○

---

3   <u>This</u> <u>snach</u> was a good <u>idea</u>.
  ○ ○   ○

---

4   Hang your <u>coat</u> in the <u>haull</u> <u>closet</u>.
     ○   ○ ○

GO ➡

5 Kurt's arm is <u>sore</u> from <u>throwing</u> too <u>heard</u>.
○ ○ ○

6 <u>These</u> <u>dishs</u> are <u>clean</u>.
○ ○ ○

7 The <u>ticket</u> to the <u>game</u> costs a <u>dolar</u>.
○ ○ ○

8 He told the <u>truth</u> about the <u>broken</u> <u>wendow</u>.
○ ○ ○

9 My <u>friends</u> <u>somtimes</u> act <u>silly</u>.
○ ○ ○

10 <u>Whare</u> is your <u>other</u> <u>boot</u>?
○ ○ ○

STOP

SAMPLE A

> Why are we going to the <u>store.</u>

- ○ Store!
- ○ store?
- ○ The way it is

SAMPLE B

> Those squirrels <u>are</u> very fast.

- ○ was
- ○ is
- ○ The way it is

1 When are you coming to visit, <u>aunt Carla?</u>

- ○ Aunt Carla?
- ○ aunt Carla!
- ○ The way it is

3 <u>Mr. Ernster, the artist,</u> signed the picture.

- ○ Mr. Ernster, the Artist,
- ○ Mr Ernster, the artist,
- ○ The way it is

2 Our band's song <u>were</u> very short.

- ○ are
- ○ was
- ○ The way it is

4 <u>your friend,</u>

What is the <u>best</u> way to write this ending of a letter?

- ○ Your friend,
- ○ your Friend,
- ○ The way it is

GO ➡

5 I <u>dont</u> want to see that movie.

○ do'nt

○ don't

○ The way it is

6 Hey, Cary! Watch out for the <u>ball?</u>

○ ball!

○ Ball.

○ The way it is

7 Our first snowstorm this year was in <u>october.</u>

○ October.

○ October?

○ The way it is

8 My apartment is the first one on the second <u>floor.</u>

○ floor?

○ floor!

○ The way it is

9 The clown <u>gived Sandra</u> a red balloon.

○ gave Sandra

○ gived sandra

○ The way it is

10 My uncle took us camping on <u>Larch mountain.</u>

○ Larch Mountain?

○ Larch Mountain.

○ The way it is

11 Joshua's cousins live in <u>Chicago Illinois.</u>

○ chicago, illinois.

○ Chicago, Illinois.

○ The way it is

12 Have you ever ridden on a <u>horse?</u>

○ horse!

○ horse.

○ The way it is

GO ➡

The team's practice will <u>start soon?</u>

○ start Soon?

○ start soon.

○ The way it is

 I was so happy when my grandmother <u>sends</u> me a card.

○ sent

○ is sending

○ The way it is

 Layla walked to <u>School with Haley.</u>

○ school with Haley.

○ School with haley.

○ The way it is

16 <u>"Laura's Wish"</u> is a very interesting story.

○ "laura's wish"

○ "Laura's wish"

○ The way it is

SAMPLE C

The car parked. At the curb.

○ The car parking at the curb.

○ The car parked at the curb.

○ The way it is

SAMPLE D

The bird hopped onto the branch.

○ The bird hopped. Onto the branch.

○ The bird hopping onto the branch.

○ The way it is

 The timer on the oven ringing.

○ The timer on the oven rang.

○ The timer on the oven. It rang.

○ The way it is

GO ➡

18 Ducks swim in the river near my house.

- ○ Ducks swim in the river. Near my house.
- ○ Ducks swim. In the river near my house.
- ○ The way it is

19 Students drawing pictures about their visit to the park.

- ○ Students drew pictures about their visit. To the park.
- ○ Students drew pictures about their visit to the park.
- ○ The way it is

20 My mother is a teacher at the school down the street.

- ○ My mother is a teacher. At the school down the street.
- ○ My mother being a teacher at the school down the street.
- ○ The way it is

21 At the zoo. Will learned about elephants.

- ○ At the zoo, Will learned about elephants.
- ○ At the zoo, Will learning about elephants.
- ○ The way it is

22 Because it was Tuesday. I went to music class after school.

- ○ Because it was Tuesday, I going to music class after school.
- ○ Because it was Tuesday, I went to music class after school.
- ○ The way it is

23 The dog saw the squirrel and barked.

- ○ The dog saw the squirrel. And barked.
- ○ The dog seeing the squirrel and barking.
- ○ The way it is

GO ➡

24 My clothes were soaked.
By the hard rain.

- ○ My clothes being soaked by the hard rain.
- ○ My clothes were soaked by the hard rain.
- ○ The way it is

25 Sam's parents sing in a band. With their friends.

- ○ Sam's parents they sing in a band with their friends.
- ○ Sam's parents sing in a band with their friends.
- ○ The way it is

26 Kyle asked a question and waited for the answer.

- ○ Kyle asked a question. Waiting for the answer.
- ○ Kyle asking a question. He waited for the answer.
- ○ The way it is

STOP

SAMPLES

Fish can live in saltwater or freshwater. Saltwater fish live in oceans or seas. If water is too salty, then no fish can live in it. Freshwater fish live in rivers and lakes. Some fish, like salmon, spend part of their lives in saltwater and part in freshwater.

SAMPLE E

Which of these would go <u>best</u> after the last sentence?

○ No matter where fish live, the water has to be clean.

○ Fish come in thousands of different shapes and sizes.

○ Did you know that some lakes are salty?

SAMPLE F

Why was this story written?

○ To tell about oceans

○ To tell where fish live

○ To tell about salmon

Story 1

Early one morning, I heard a shout from outside. It was snowing. I put on a coat and went out to play with my neighbors. We jumped and slid in the thin layer of snow. All morning we played in the slushy snow.

GO ➡

27 Which of these would go <u>best</u> after the last sentence?

○ I like playing with my neighbors.

○ Each snowflake has a different pattern.

○ We had fun until the snow melted.

 28 Which of these would <u>not</u> go with this story?

○ There wasn't enough snow to make a snowman.

○ My neighbor, Colin, likes to go skiing when it snows.

○ It doesn't snow around here very often.

Story 2

When Kevin gets to the beach, he rushes over the sand to the high tide mark. That's where the waves leave a big pile of seaweed. Kevin likes to poke through the pile. He finds shells and pieces of driftwood.

 29 Which of these would go <u>best</u> after the last sentence?

○ One time Kevin found a glass float from a fishing net.

○ Each high tide leaves its own mark on the beach.

○ Kevin's sisters like to build sand castles.

 30 Which of these would <u>not</u> go with this story?

○ Sometimes the seaweed smells bad, but he doesn't care.

○ Seaweed is food for some of the animals in the ocean.

○ The driftwood he finds is smooth and silvery.

GO ➡

Story 3

The car was packed. Mom said, "Load up!" and everyone climbed in. Ben watched out the window as they passed trees and fields. All day the family drove. At night, they set up their tent. Ben stared at the stars. "I like this trip," he said.

---

 31 Why was this story written?

○ To tell how far a family drove

○ To tell about a trip

○ To tell why Ben likes camping

---

 32 Which of these would go <u>best</u> after the last sentence?

○ Ben hoped they could go camping again.

○ Ben got tired of sitting still in the car.

○ Mom and Dad sang songs while they drove.

---

 33 Which of these would <u>not</u> go with this story?

○ The tent fell over twice before they got it right.

○ Ben's dad had just taught him how to swim.

○ The car was full of sleeping bags and folding chairs.

GO ➡

Story 4

Aunt Sophie likes music. She wants to play the guitar, so she is taking lessons. She practices all the time, and she can already play songs. She taught me the words so I can sing along.

 34 Which of these would go <u>best</u> after the last sentence?

- ○ Her teacher says that practice is very important.
- ○ Aunt Sophie likes to dance to music on the radio.
- ○ Aunt Sophie and I have fun making music together.

 36 Which of these would <u>not</u> go with this story?

- ○ I like singing while Aunt Sophie plays.
- ○ Some of the songs have words.
- ○ Aunt Sophie lives a few blocks away.

 35 Why was this story written?

- ○ To tell how to play a guitar
- ○ To tell what Aunt Sophie learned to do
- ○ To tell what songs Aunt Sophie likes

STOP

SAMPLE G

> Reena is making a shopping list for the grocery store.

Which of these does <u>not</u> belong on her list?

- ○ Milk
- ○ Bread
- ○ Radio

SAMPLE H

> Bart is writing a story about making cookies.

Which idea should be first?

- ○ Eating the tasty cookies
- ○ Mixing everything together
- ○ Putting the cookies in the oven

 37

> Peggy is writing a letter to a friend describing her town park.

Which of these belongs in her letter?

- ○ The kinds of trees in the park
- ○ The street names in her town
- ○ The weather this time of year

38

> Arnie wants to invite some friends to his house for a party.

Which idea does <u>not</u> belong in the invitation?

- ○ When the party will take place
- ○ The reason for the party
- ○ Arnie's favorite baseball team

STOP

SAMPLE A
- ○ dress
- ○ feed
- ○ wash

SAMPLE B
- ○ warn
- ○ call
- ○ trick

1
- ○ teeth
- ○ hair
- ○ tail

2
- ○ find
- ○ empty
- ○ mix

3
- ○ listen to it
- ○ look at it
- ○ yell at it

4
- ○ wet
- ○ green
- ○ short

5
- ○ tidy
- ○ small
- ○ whole

6
- ○ run
- ○ trip
- ○ hike

GO

SAMPLE C

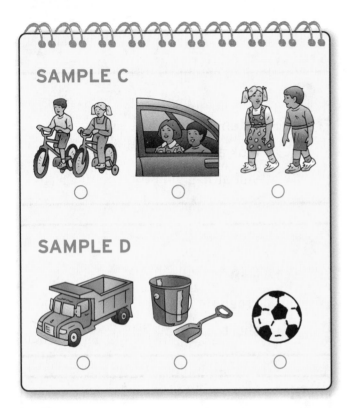

SAMPLE D

7

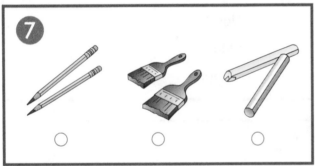

8

9

10

11

GO ➡

SAMPLE E

- ○ Dog
- ○ Cat
- ○ Rabbit

SAMPLE F

- ○ To a bush
- ○ To a lake
- ○ To a nest
- ○ To a roof

12

- ○ Its parts are easy to find.
- ○ You can make it by yourself.
- ○ It is easy to play.

13

- ○ drum
- ○ whistle
- ○ rattle

14

- ○ They will not cut the plastic.
- ○ They make better sound.
- ○ They will not hurt your hands.

15

- ○ A gas mask
- ○ A car
- ○ A printing machine

16

- ○ where leafcutter ants live
- ○ how leafcutter ants fight
- ○ what leafcutter ants eat
- ○ how leafcutter ants build nests

17

- ○ give directions
- ○ tell a story
- ○ give information
- ○ explain about farming

GO ➡

18
- ○ "Kareem Makes a Cake"
- ○ "Kareem's Recipe"
- ○ "Louis Learns to Cook"
- ○ "Louis's Idea"

19
- ○ yogurt
- ○ a sandwich
- ○ a snack
- ○ granola

20
- ○ A cup
- ○ A pan
- ○ A jar
- ○ A bowl

21
- ○ simple
- ○ difficult
- ○ scary
- ○ funny

22
- ○ helpful
- ○ friendly
- ○ careful
- ○ silly

23
- ○ took his mom's mail
- ○ put on his raincoat
- ○ stepped in puddles
- ○ wrote a letter

24
- ○ His mother made a treat for him.
- ○ The mail carrier came to his house.
- ○ Mr. Hong wrote to him.
- ○ The rain stopped.

25
- ○ a friend
- ○ his daughter
- ○ a teacher
- ○ his brother

STOP